Zaner-Bloser

Handwriting

Author

Clinton S. Hackney, Ed.D.

Reviewers

Julie Althide, Teacher, Hazelwood School District, St. Louis, Missouri

Becky Brashears, Teacher, Gocio Elementary, Sarasota, Florida

Douglas Dewey, Teacher, National Heritage Academies, Grand Rapids, Michigan

Jennifer B. Dutcher, Teacher, Elk Grove School District, Sacramento, California

Gita Farbman, Teacher, School District of Philadelphia, Philadelphia, Pennsylvania

Susan Ford, Teacher, St. Ann's School, Charlotte, North Carolina

Brenda Forehand, Teacher, David Lipscomb Middle School, Nashville, Tennessee

Sharon Hall, Teacher, USD 443, Dodge City, Kansas

Sr. James Madeline, Teacher, St. Anthony School, Allston, Massachusetts

Lori A. Martin, Teacher, Chicago Public Schools, Chicago, Illinois

Vikki F. McCurdy, Teacher, Mustang School District, Oklahoma City, Oklahoma

Melissa Neary Morgan, Reading Specialist, Fairfax County Public Schools, Fairfax, Virginia

Sue Postlewait, Literacy Resource Consultant, Marshall County Schools, Moundsville, West Virginia

Gloria C. Rivera, Principal, Edinburg CISO, Edinburg, Texas

Rebecca Rollefson, Teacher, Ericsson Community School, Minneapolis, Minnesota

Susan Samsa, Teacher, Dover City Schools, Dover, Ohio

Zelda J. Smith, Instructional Specialist, New Orleans Public Schools, New Orleans, Louisiana

Occupational Therapy Consultant: Maureen E. King, O.T.R.

Credits

Art: John Hovell: 14, 29, 34, 69, 70, 71, 78; Tom Leonard: 4, 5, 11, 13, 23, 26, 45, 52, 53, 73, 74, 75, 76; Jane McCreary: 3, 19, 54, 64, 65; Sharron O'Neil: 3, 24, 49, 62; Andy San Diego: 56, 59

Photos: George C. Anderson Photography, Inc.: 4

Literature: "This Land Is Your Land." Words and Music by Woody Guthrie. TRO-© Copyright 1956 (Renewed), 1958 (Renewed) and 1970 Ludlow Music, Inc., New York, NY. Used by Permission.

Development: Kirchoff/Wohlberg, Inc., in collaboration with Zaner-Bloser Educational Publishers

ISBN 0-7367-1215-1

05 06 159 5

Zaner-Bloser, Inc., P.O. Box 16764, Columbus, Ohio 43216-6764
1-800-421-3018
www.zaner-bloser.com
Printed in the United States of America

Contents

A Frontier Tale

Lincoln Elementary Fifth Grade Play

Place: the Oregon wilderness, around 1845

Act One

Scene One

Sarah Shaw (a pioneer): We've been traveling for months now, since the spring when we left Boston to come West.

Johnson (a trapper): It's a wide-open country, with plenty of land for everyone.

You write for many reasons at school, at home, and in your community. The lessons in this book will help you write legibly so you and other people can easily read what you have written.

Evaluating your own handwriting is a good habit to form. When you see the **Stop and Check** sign in this book, stop and circle the best letter or joining you wrote on that line.

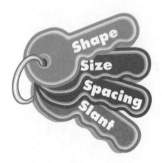

You will see the **Keys to Legibility** throughout this book. They will help you remember to check the **shape, size, spacing,** and **slant** of your writing to make sure it is easy to read.

4

On another piece of paper, write the first stanza of this American folk song in your best cursive handwriting.

Circle your three best letters. Underline three letters that need improvement.

This Land Is Your Land

This land is your land,
this land is my land
From California to the New York
island,
From the redwood forest to the
Gulf Stream waters   STOP
This land was made
for you and me.

As I was walking that ribbon
of highway,
I saw above me that endless
skyway,
I saw below me that golden
valley
This land was made for you
and me.

Woody Guthrie

5

Writing Positions and Basic Strokes

Sit comfortably with your feet flat on the floor.
Rest both arms on the desk. Shift your paper as you write.

Paper Position

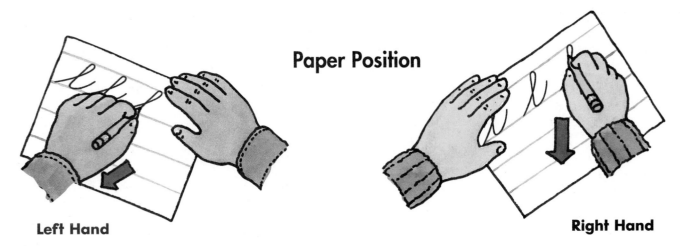

Left Hand

Right Hand

Pencil Position

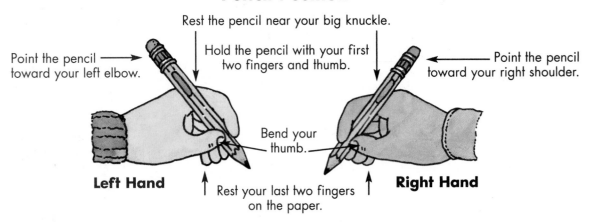

Rest the pencil near your big knuckle.

Point the pencil toward your left elbow.

Hold the pencil with your first two fingers and thumb.

Point the pencil toward your right shoulder.

Bend your thumb.

Left Hand

Right Hand

Rest your last two fingers on the paper.

Practice the basic cursive strokes.

Undercurve

Downcurve

Overcurve

Slant

Cursive Letters and Numerals

Aa Bb Cc Dd Ee Ff Gg
Hh Ii Jj Kk Ll Mm
Nn Oo Pp Qq Rr Ss Tt
Uu Vv Ww Xx Yy Zz
1 2 3 4 5 6 7 8 9 10

Write your full name.
_____

Write the name of your school, its street address, and the city and state.
_____
_____
_____

Write your date of birth and your age.
_____

Write the title of your favorite book or song.
_____
_____

Write the letters and numerals you like best to write.
_____
_____
_____

Keys to Legibility

Shape

As you write cursive, pay attention to the shape of your letters. Using good basic strokes will improve the shape of your letters.

undercurve strokes	∕	t	$\mathcal{S}$	j	w
downcurve strokes	(	g	a	o	c
overcurve strokes	(	v	y	n	$\mathcal{J}$
slant strokes	∕	K	f	d	$\mathcal{U}$

Size

You should also pay attention to the size of your writing.

Tall letters do not touch the headline.

Some lowercase letters are tall letters.

d k f l

All uppercase letters are tall letters.

J a S $\mathcal{L}$

Numerals are the height of tall letters.

0 5 9 3

Short letters are half the height of tall letters.

Many lowercase letters are short letters.

c v m a

Descenders do not go too far below the baseline.

Some lowercase letters have descenders.

g p y j

Some uppercase letters have descenders.

f Y z j

Practice
Write Homophones

Write each sentence. Then, circle two words that sound alike but have different spellings and meanings.

1. Use the oar, or you'll just float.

2. Jan ate all eight pieces of pizza.

3. The patients had much patience.

4. The crews worked on the cruise.

5. I read the red book while waiting.

6. What a cute pale blue pail!

7. Our math class lasts for an hour.

8. Some of us knew the sum.

9. Close the clothes closet door.

10. Sandpaper is coarse, of course!

Keys to Legibility

My writing has good shape. ☐
My writing has good size. ☐

Manuscript Maintenance

Compound Words

A compound word is made up of two words that come together to form a single word. Fill in the missing letters to complete each compound word in the puzzle. Use manuscript writing.

tumbleweeds	seaside	waterway
landform	farmhouse	newspaper
stagecoach	postmaster	northwestern

		_	_	_	_	_	_	w	e	e	d	s
												t
		n	e	w	s	_	_	_	_	_		a
		_										g
		_		f	a	r	m	_	_	_	_	e
		_										_
		_										_
		w	_	_	_	_	w	a	y			_
		e										_
p	o	s	t	_	_	_	_	_	_			_
		t										
	s	e	a	_	_	_	_					
		r										
_	_	n	_	f	o	r	m					

Writing Legibly

I. Study these tips for legible writing. They will help you avoid common handwriting errors when you write.

✓ Close letters that should be closed. Write d, not cl.

✓ Keep checkstrokes at the right height. Write σ, not a.

✓ When letters have loops that go below the baseline, close the loop at the baseline. Write g, not g.

2. Look at this part of a student's math story problem. Underline letters that need improvement.

> Ryan invited sixteen friends to a mid-week pizza party. Each pizza has eight slices. How many pizzas are needed so that the serving for each guest equals four slices?

3. Rewrite the student's problem correctly, then write a math story problem of your own. Pay attention to the tips for legible writing.

Write Overcurve Letters

Write the letters, joinings, and words.

n   *n*   *n*   *n*   *n*   *n*   *n*

ni   *nu*   *no*   *na*   *nn*   *ny*

naturalist   *number*   *nightfall*

noontime   *announce*   *funny*

m   *m*   *m*   *m*   *m*   *m*   *m*

mi   *me*   *ma*   *mo*   *mn*

mainland   *mobile*   *menu*

microscope   *millimeter*   *autumn*

Undercurve to Downcurve Joining

The undercurve swings up and over to form the top of the downcurve letter.

ma not *ma*

✔ Check your writing folder for undercurve joinings that need improvement.

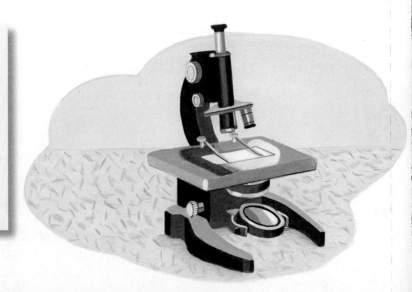

26

Write the letters, joinings, and words.

y   y   y   y   y   y   y

ye   ys   yt   ya   yo   ym

yard   yesterday   yoke

myth   physical   gymnast

x   x   x   x   x   x   x

xp   xt   xi   xa   xc   xy

expand   galaxy   texture

exist   exactly   exciting

Undercurve to Downcurve Joining

The undercurve swings up and over to form the top
of the downcurve letter. Remember to cross **x** after
the word is finished.

xc   not   xu

✔ Check your writing folder for undercurve joinings
that need improvement.

Slant

Circle three words you wrote
that have good slant.

27

Write Overcurve Letters

Write the letters, joinings, and words.

v   *v*   *v*   *v*   *v*   *v*   *v*

ve   *vi*   *vo*   *va*   *vy*

vice-president   *vow*   *value*

adventure   *wavy*   *arrive*

z   *z*   *z*   *z*   *z*   *z*   *z*

ze   *zi*   *zo*   *za*   *zy*   *zz*

zigzag   *zone*   *zaniest*

lazy   *pretzel*   *dizziness*

Overcurve to Overcurve Joining

The overcurve ending turns quickly into the overcurve stroke of the following letter.

zy   not   *zy*

✔ Check your writing folder for overcurve joinings that need improvement.

Slant

Circle three letters you wrote that have good slant.

Practice
Alliterative Phrases

The words in each phrase begin with the same sound.
This is called alliteration.

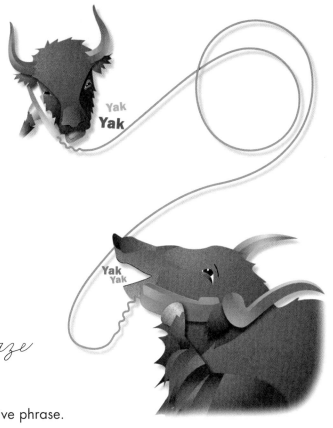

Yak
Yak

Yak
Yak

yak-yak

perfectly plain pasta

zigzagging zebras

neat notebook notes

velvety voices

mysterious meandering maze

Write a sentence to answer each question. Use an alliterative phrase.

1. What animal talks too much?

2. What is easy to read?

3. Where might you get lost?

4. What is spaghetti with no sauce?

5. What are black and white inline skaters?

6. What does a smooth-sounding singing group have?

Keys to Legibility

Shape
Size
Spacing
Slant

My writing has good shape. ☐
My writing has good size. ☐
My writing has good spacing. ☐
My writing has good slant. ☐

29

Manuscript Maintenance

Being a Wordsmith

A **wordsmith** is a person who works with words. Now it's your turn to be a wordsmith.
See how many words you can write using only the letters **w, o, r, d, s, m, i, t,** and **h**.
You may use each letter more than once. Write in manuscript.

wordsmith

_____   _____

_____   _____

_____   _____

_____   _____

_____   _____

_____   _____

The next word to try is **handwriting**.
See how many words you can write using the letters **h, a, n, d, w, r, i, t,** and **g**.
You may use each letter more than once. Write in manuscript.

handwriting

_____   _____

_____   _____

_____   _____

_____   _____

_____   _____

Writing Legibly

I. Study these tips for legible writing. They will help you avoid common handwriting errors when you write.

✔ When letters have loops that go below the baseline, close the loop at the baseline. Write *z*, not *z* .

✔ Keep checkstrokes at the right height. Write *v*, not *u* .

✔ Make sure curves are smooth and rounded. Write *m*, not *m* .

✔ Begin overcurve letters with an overcurve. Write *x*, not *x* .

2. Look at a part of this student's health report. Underline letters that need improvement.

> Eating balanced meals is one way
> to keep healthy. Some people take
> extra vitamins and enzymes for
> added nutrition. Regular exercise
> is also important.

3. Rewrite the report correctly, then write part of a report you have written. Pay attention to the tips for legible writing.

Write Downcurve Letters

Write the letters, joinings, and words.

a

a a a a a a a

Al   Ap   Ad   Ag   An   Am

Alamo   Adirondacks   America

Anasazi   Appalachia   Andover

O

O O O O O O O

Oklahoma   Oregon   Omaha

Orlando   Ocean City   Oakland

DID YOU KNOW?

Akron is a city in Ohio.

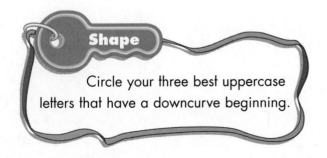

JOINING ALERT

a is joined to the letter that follows.

O is not joined to the letter that follows.

Ad not Od

The undercurve to downcurve joining becomes a doublecurve. At the end of the doublecurve, you retrace.

Shape

Circle your three best uppercase letters that have a downcurve beginning.

32

Write the letters, joinings, and words.

$\mathcal{D}$ $\mathcal{D}$ $\mathcal{D}$ $\mathcal{D}$ $\mathcal{D}$ $\mathcal{D}$ $\mathcal{D}$ $\mathcal{D}$ $\mathcal{D}$

Dallas   Des Moines   Dover

Dodge City   Douglas   Davis

$\mathcal{C}$ $\mathcal{C}$ $\mathcal{C}$ $\mathcal{C}$ $\mathcal{C}$ $\mathcal{C}$ $\mathcal{C}$ $\mathcal{C}$

Ce   Ch   Ci   Ca   Co   Cy

Catskills   Chicago   Cypress

$\mathcal{E}$ $\mathcal{E}$ $\mathcal{E}$ $\mathcal{E}$ $\mathcal{E}$ $\mathcal{E}$ $\mathcal{E}$ $\mathcal{E}$

Er   El   Ea   Ed   En   Em

Earhart   Encinitas   Ericson

JOINING ALERT

$\mathcal{D}$ is not joined to the letter that follows.

$\mathcal{C}$ and $\mathcal{E}$ are joined to the letter that follows.

En not *En*

The undercurve swings wide, then overcurves quickly into the slant stroke.

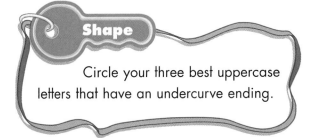

Shape

Circle your three best uppercase letters that have an undercurve ending.

33

Practice
Ocean Facts

Write these facts about oceans.

1. The earth has four oceans.

2. Oceans cover about 70 percent of Earth.

3. Climates are affected by oceans.

4. Earth's oceans flow into each other.

5. Many ships sail across the Atlantic.

6. Deepest of the four is the Pacific.

7. The Arctic is the smallest ocean.

8. The Indian Ocean touches four of Earth's continents.

BONUS
Can you name the four continents that touch the Indian Ocean?

Keys to Legibility

My writing has good shape. ☐

Manuscript Maintenance

Yearbook Entry

Your class is going to publish a yearbook.
Under each student's picture will be some information about that student.
Fill out the form below for your entry in the yearbook. Write in manuscript.

First Name:

Grade:

School:

Favorite subject:

Favorite sport or hobby:

What I like best about school:

What I like to do after school:

Favorite book:

Favorite movie:

Write Curve Forward Letters

Write the letters, joinings, and words.

n   n   n   n   n   n   n   n

Ne   Ni   Nu   Na   No   Ny

New Jersey   North Dakota

Nashville   New Orleans   Nome

m   m   m   m   m   m   m   m

Mi   Mu   Me   Mo   Ma   My

Montana   Minnesota   Missouri

Maryland   Myrtle Beach

JOINING ALERT

n and m are joined to the letter that follows.

Ne not Ne   Me not Me

The undercurve joining must be wide enough to allow room for the loop in **e**.

Size

Circle your three best tall letters.

Write the letters, joinings, and words.

H   H   H   H   H   H   H

Hi   He   Hu   Ha   Ho   Hy

Harlem   Houston   Hiram

Hancock   High Plains   Hamilton

K   K   K   K   K   K   K

Ki   Ke   Ka   Ko   Kn   Ky

Kansas   Kentucky   Kitty Hawk

Key West   Knoxville   Kokomo

JOINING ALERT

H and K are joined to the letter that follows.

He not He

The loop in **H** swings across the letter and slightly down to make room for the loop in **e**.

Size

Circle your three best tall letters.

Write Curve Forward Letters

Write the letters, joinings, and words.

𝒰   𝒰   𝒰   𝒰   𝒰   𝒰   𝒰

Ut   Ur   Ua   Ug   Um   Un

The United States   Utah

The United Nations   Urbana

𝒴   𝒴   𝒴   𝒴   𝒴   𝒴   𝒴

Ye   Yi   Yu   Yo   Ya

Youngstown   Yorktown   Yukon

Yosemite   Yellowstone   Yuma

JOINING ALERT

𝒰 and 𝒴 are joined to the letter that follows.

Ya not Ya

The overcurve ending crosses at the baseline, then continues up and wide to form the downcurve letter.

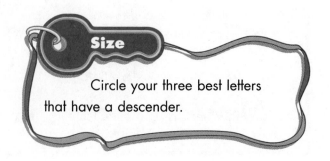

Size

Circle your three best letters that have a descender.

38

Write the letters, joinings, and words.

Z   Z   Z   Z   Z   Z   Z   Z

Zu   Ze   Zh   Za   Zo   Zy

Zanesville   Zurich   Zuni

New Zealand   Zion National Park

V   V   V   V   V   V   V   V

Vallejo   Virginia   Vermont

Vicksburg   Valley Forge   Vista

DID YOU KNOW?

Mount Vernon is in Virginia.

JOINING ALERT

Z is joined to the letter that follows.
V is not joined to the letter that follows.

Zo not Zo

The overcurve ending crosses at the baseline, then
continues up and wide to form the downcurve letter.

Size

Circle your three best letters
that have a descender.

Write Curve Forward Letters

Write the letters and words.

W W W W W W W W

West Virginia   Washington

Mt. Whitney   Williamsburg

X X X X X X X X

Xenia   Xanthus   Xenon

Xalapa, Mexico   Xapuri, Brazil

DID YOU KNOW?

Washington is a west-coast state.

JOINING ALERT

W is not joined to the letter that follows.

Joining *X* is optional.

Xe   Xe

Unjoined   **Joined**

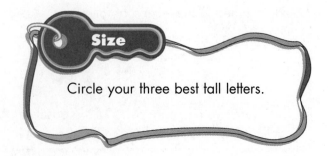

Size

Circle your three best tall letters.

Names of States

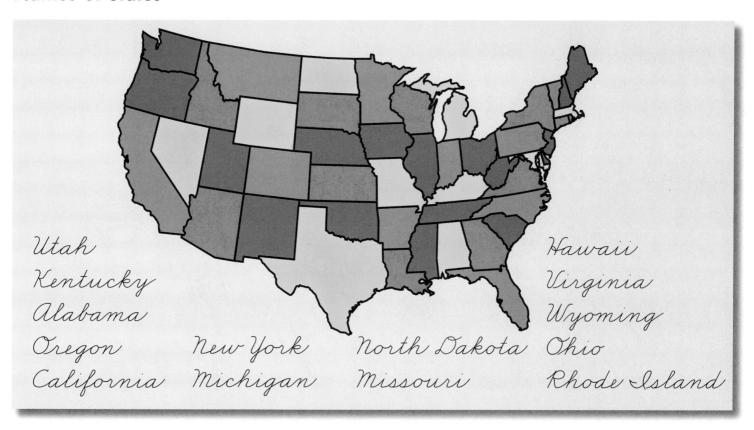

Utah
Kentucky
Alabama
Oregon
California

New York
Michigan

North Dakota
Missouri

Hawaii
Virginia
Wyoming
Ohio
Rhode Island

Write these names of states under the correct heading. Use your best cursive writing.

Names with fewer than 8 letters

Names with 8 letters or more

BONUS
Which state is known as the "Show-Me State"?

Keys to Legibility

My writing has good shape. ☐
My writing has good size. ☐

Writing Legibly

I. Study these tips for legible writing. They will help you avoid common handwriting errors when you write.

- ✔ Write strokes carefully. Write K, not K .
- ✔ Close letters that should be closed. Write a, not a .
- ✔ Don't add loops to letters that should not be looped. Write y, not y .
- ✔ Make sure all uppercase letters are tall. Write M, not m .

2. Look at this section from a student's history paper. Underline letters that need improvement.

> Are you curious about faraway galaxies? In 1803, Thomas Jefferson was curious about the unexplored West. He asked Meriwether Lewis and William Clark to go and learn all they could about the land between the Mississippi River and the Pacific Ocean.

3. Rewrite the student's paper correctly, or write a section from one of your own papers. Pay attention to the tips for legible writing.

Write Overcurve Letters

Write the letters, joinings, and words.

$\mathcal{I}$ $\mathcal{I}$ $\mathcal{I}$ $\mathcal{I}$ $\mathcal{I}$ $\mathcal{I}$ $\mathcal{I}$ ✓

Indiana   Idaho   Illinois

$\mathcal{J}$ $\mathcal{J}$ $\mathcal{J}$ $\mathcal{J}$ $\mathcal{J}$ $\mathcal{J}$ $\mathcal{J}$ ✓

Ji   Je   Ju   Jo   Ja   Jy ✓

Jackson   Jamestown   Juneau

Q Q Q Q Q Q Q ✓

Quanah   Quakertown   Quimby

DID YOU KNOW?

Quanah is a city in Texas.

JOINING ALERT

$\mathcal{J}$ is joined to the letter that follows.

Q is not joined to the letter that follows.

Joining $\mathcal{I}$ to the letter that follows is optional.

In   In

Unjoined   **Joined**

Spacing

Circle your three best joinings.

Write Doublecurve Letters

Write the letters and words.

T *T* *T* *T* *T* *T* *T* ✓

Tallahassee   Texas   Tetons

Lake Tahoe   Tucson   Tacoma

F *F* *F* *F* *F* *F* *F* ✓

Fairfax   Fort Sumter   Fulton

Franklin   Fitchburg   Flagstaff

DID YOU KNOW?

The Everglades are in Florida.

Florida and Texas are in the South.

JOINING ALERT

Joining *T* and *F* is optional.

Ty   Fa   *Ty   Fa*

Unjoined   **Joined**

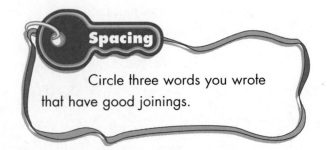

Spacing

Circle three words you wrote that have good joinings.

Practice
The Early Presidents

Write the names of the first ten Presidents of the United States.

1. *George Washington*

2. *John Adams*

3. *Thomas Jefferson*

4. *James Madison*

5. *James Monroe*

6. *John Quincy Adams*

7. *Andrew Jackson*

8. *Martin Van Buren*

9. *William Henry Harrison*

10. *John Tyler*

BONUS
How many U.S. Presidents have the name "John"?

Keys to Legibility

My writing has good shape. ☐
My writing has good size. ☐
My writing has good spacing. ☐

45

Manuscript Maintenance

A Number Code

1 A	2 B	3 C	4 D	5 E	6 F	7 G	8 H	9 I	10 J	11 K	12 L	13 M
14 N	15 O	16 P	17 Q	18 R	19 S	20 T	21 U	22 V	23 W	24 X	25 Y	26 Z

Each number in the code stands for a letter.
Decode each riddle and its answer. Write in uppercase manuscript.

```
____  ____  __  ____    __  ____  __  ____
 23    8    1   20      4   15    5   19
                                        ?
__  __  ____  __  ____  __  ____  __
 4   5   12   1   23    1   18    5
                                          !
__  ____  __  ____    ____  __  ____  ____  __  ____
 1   14   5   23      10    5   18    19    5   25
```

```
____  __  __  ____  __    __  __  ____
 23    8   5   18   5     8   1   19
                           ?
____  ____  __  __  ____  ____
 15    18   5   7   15    14
                                          !
____  ____    ____  ____  ____  __  __  ____  ____  __
 20    15     15    11    12    1   8   15    13    1
```

Write a message using the code.

_____

_____

Write Undercurve-Loop Letters

Write the letters and words.

G G G G G G G

Gettysburg   Grand Rapids   Gary

Great Bend   Rio Grande   Gallup

S S S S S S S

South Dakota   South Carolina

Salem   Savannah   Seattle

L L L L L L L

Lafayette   Louisiana   Lansing

Lake Erie   Lexington   Lima

JOINING ALERT

L is not joined to the letter that follows.
Joining *G* and *S* is optional.

Go   Sa   Go   Sa

Unjoined   **Joined**

Slant

Circle three letters you wrote that have good slant.

Write Undercurve-Slant Letters

Write the letters, joinings, and words.

P   P   P   P   P   P   P   P   ✓

Pennsylvania   Philadelphia

Palo Alto   The Pacific Palisades

R   R   R   R   R   R   R   R   ✓

Rh   Re   Ri   Ra   Ro   Ry   ✓

Raleigh   Rhode Island   Reno

B   B   B   B   B   B   B   B   ✓

Boston   Boise   Bunker Hill

Boonesville   Bowie   Buffalo

JOINING ALERT

R is joined to the letter that follows.

P is not joined to the letter that follows.

Joining B is optional.

Ba   Ba
Unjoined   **Joined**

Slant

Circle three words you wrote that have good slant.

Practice
National Parks

Rocky Mountain, Colorado
Bryce Canyon, Utah
Glacier, Montana
Lake Clark, Alaska
Shenandoah, Virginia
Sequoia, Arizona
Redwood, California
Petrified Forest, Arizona
Grand Canyon, Arizona
Big Bend, Texas

Write the names of national parks you can visit in each of these states.

California

Colorado

Texas

Virginia

Montana

Utah

Arizona

Alaska

Keys to Legibility

Shape
Size
Spacing
Slant

My writing has good shape. ☐
My writing has good size. ☐
My writing has good spacing. ☐
My writing has good slant. ☐

Writing Legibly

When you edit and proofread your writing, do you remember to check your handwriting? Taking time to make sure your handwriting is legible shows courtesy to your readers. It also helps you keep your handwriting skills sharp. Follow these steps for writing legibly.

I. Study tips for legible writing. The **Keys to Legibility** are easy to remember. They tell you what qualities to look for in your handwriting.

✓ Each letter should have good **Shape**.

Write *b*, not *b* . Write *e*, not *e* .

✓ Make sure letters are the proper **Size**. Tall letters should be twice the height of short letters.

Write *Adam*, not *Adam* .

✓ Check for good **Spacing**. Leave space for *○* between letters, space for ** between words, and space for *○* between sentences.

Write *Check the chalkboard*, not

Check the chalkboard .

✓ Keep your **Slant** uniform.

Write *f*, not *f* .

2. Look closely at your handwriting. Underline places that need improvement in this student's story beginning.

> *A rainy day found my cousin Robin and me stuck inside at our aunt's house. We got bored just hanging around playing video games. "Let's explore the basement of this old house," Robin said. I agreed. Down the damp, crumbling steps we went, brushing cobwebs from our faces. Thick dust lay over boxes, jars, and strange artifacts stacked on leaning shelves.*

"Hey, what's this?" Robin shouted, making my shoulders shake with fright.

"It looks like a door," I said as I knelt to open the rotting square of wood on rusty hinges.

"It's some kind of passageway," Robin guessed. "Let's check it out."

3. Rewrite, correcting the mistakes you found. On the lines below, rewrite the story beginning, then continue the story or write a story of your own.

Cursive Review

Write each joining. Then write two words that contain the joining. Use the dictionary to help you.

undercurve to undercurve	*us*
undercurve to downcurve	*ed*
undercurve to overcurve	*ny*
overcurve to undercurve	*ju*
overcurve to downcurve	*yo*
overcurve to overcurve	*zy*
checkstroke to undercurve	*br*
checkstroke to downcurve	*wa*
checkstroke to overcurve	*by*

Now write four sentences using some of the words you wrote above.

$\mathcal{A}, \mathcal{C}, \mathcal{E}, \mathcal{N}, \mathcal{M}, \mathcal{H}, \mathcal{K}, \mathcal{U}, \mathcal{Y}, \mathcal{Z}, \mathcal{J}$, and $\mathcal{R}$ are joined to the letter that follows.

$\mathcal{O}, \mathcal{D}, \mathcal{V}, \mathcal{W}, \mathcal{Q}, \mathcal{L}$, and $\mathcal{P}$ are not joined to the letter that follows.

Joining $\mathcal{X}, \mathcal{I}, \mathcal{T}, \mathcal{F}, \mathcal{G}, \mathcal{S}$, and $\mathcal{B}$ to the letter that follows is optional.

Play Geography

Write a list of place names. Each place name must begin with the last letter of the previous name.
The list is started for you.

Mississippi, Indiana, Akron,
Nome, Evanston,

Using Your Writing

Now that you have practiced writing letters, you are ready to write without models.
You'll find that the more you write in cursive, the easier and faster it will be. In the following lessons,
you'll write more and learn more about how to make your writing easy to read.

Happy Holiday! Write at least two sentences that send a holiday message to a friend.

Happy Holiday!

LEGIBLE LETTERS

Remember! Letters with good shape are easy to read.
Tall letters should not touch the headline.
Short letters should be half the height of tall letters.
Descenders should not go too far below the baseline.

People in America and around the world celebrate many holidays.
Write the names of the following holidays. Pay attention to the shape
and size of your writing.

Kwanzaa (African American Heritage Festival)

El Grito de Independencia (Mexican Independence Day)

Shogatsu (Japanese New Year)

Urini Nal (Korean Children's Day)

Do your letters have good shape?	Yes	No
Are all your tall letters the same size?	Yes	No
Are all your short letters the same size?	Yes	No

Write Research Questions

Writing research questions helps you narrow a topic and find the facts you need. Choose a state that you would like to research. Read the example questions about Michigan. Then, in the space below, write at least six research questions about the state you chose.

Michigan
1. Where is it located?
2. What is the state capital?
3. Describe the state flag.
4. What is the weather like there?
5. What is manufactured there?
6. What are the largest cities?

Do your letters have good shape?   Yes   No
Is your writing easy to read?   Yes   No

Write Titles

Underline the titles of long works, including books, magazines, newspapers, movies, and Web sites.

Books	Journeys in Time	Movies	The Patriot
Magazines	U.S. News and World Report	Web sites	www.anywebsite.com
Newspapers	The New York Times		

Use quotation marks around the titles of short works, including short stories, articles, and songs.

Short Stories	"The Story of Lewis and Clark"	Songs	"America the Beautiful"
Articles	"Florida's Great Natural Wonders"		

Write the titles. Add an underline or quotation marks to each title.

(book) *Places in Time*

(magazine) *Cobblestone*

(movie) *California, Here I Come!*

(article) *The Story of the Oregon Trail*

(song) *The Star-Spangled Banner*

(story) *The Open Window*

(Web site) *www.lookitup.com*

(newspaper) *International Herald Tribune*

Write a Business Letter

Read this business letter. Notice its six parts.

541 Lake Drive
River Forest, Illinois 60305
October 7, _____ ← heading

Washington Board of Tourism
12 Main Street, Suite 5C
Port Townsend, Washington 98368 ← inside address

Dear Tourism Director: ← greeting

I am interested in facts about Washington's
population, geography, and history. Please send
me any free information you offer. ← body

Thank you very much.
Sincerely, ← closing
Lee Hsu ← signature

Write the body of this letter in cursive, paying attention to the size and shape of your letters.

_____

_____

_____

_____

COLLISION ALERT Remember that tall letters should not touch the headline.

Do your tall letters avoid touching the headline?	Yes	No
Is your writing legible?	Yes	No

Write Notes

When you take notes from an article or book, first write the title and author.
Then write the most important facts in your own words.

Read the following passage about Florida and the notes a student wrote about it. Then write more notes about the passage. As you write, pay attention to the shape and size of your letters.

Florida's History by William Wycher

Florida has an exciting history. Juan Ponce de León, a Spanish explorer, first arrived there in 1513, in search of a mythical "fountain of youth." He didn't find the fountain, but he did find lots of flowers. The name "florida" is Spanish for "many flowers." Florida was not settled by the Spanish until 1565, when they founded St. Augustine. This city would become the United States' first permanent European settlement. In 1763, Spain gave Florida to the English. England ruled Florida until 1783, when Spain took it back. In 1821, the United States took control of "The Sunshine State."

"Florida's History" by William Wycher

1. *Ponce de León arrives in 1513 in search of "fountain of youth"*
2. *"florida" means "many flowers" in Spanish*
3.
4.

Do your letters have good shape?	Yes	No
Is your writing easy to read?	Yes	No

59

Write an Outline

An outline is a writing plan. Here is the first part of an outline for a report on the state of Virginia.

All About "Old Dominion," the State of Virginia → title
I. *Virginia's History* → main topic
   A. *First Settlers* → subtopic
      1. *Iroquoian and Algonquian Indians* → detail
      2. *English settlers at Jamestown, 1607* → detail
   B. *American Revolution*

Use the details below to complete the outline. Pay attention to the shape and size of your letters.

Shenandoah National Park   President George Washington   Meriwether Lewis
Jefferson's home at Monticello   President Thomas Jefferson   William Clark

II. *Virginia's Tourist Attractions*
   A. *National Parks*
      1. *Jamestown Festival Park* _____
      2. _____

   B. *General Attractions*
      1. *Colonial Williamsburg* _____
      2. _____

III. *Famous Virginians*
   A. *Explorers* _____
      1. _____
      2. _____

   B. *Leaders* _____
      1. _____
      2. _____

Size

Are all your tall letters the same size?	Yes	No
Do your descenders avoid crashing into the letters below?	Yes	No

60

Write a Paragraph

A paragraph is a group of sentences related to a main idea.
The following sentences make up a paragraph.
Notice that the first line is indented.

> *Many famous people come from Virginia, especially explorers and politicians. For example, explorers Meriwether Lewis and William Clark were born in Virginia. George Washington and Thomas Jefferson, two United States presidents, were also born in Virginia.*

Write the paragraph. Pay attention to the shape and size of your letters.

_____

_____

_____

_____

_____

_____

_____

_____

DID YOU KNOW?

Richmond is the capital of Virginia.

	Do your letters have good shape?	Yes	No
	Is your writing easy to read?	Yes	No

Manuscript Maintenance

Write Labels

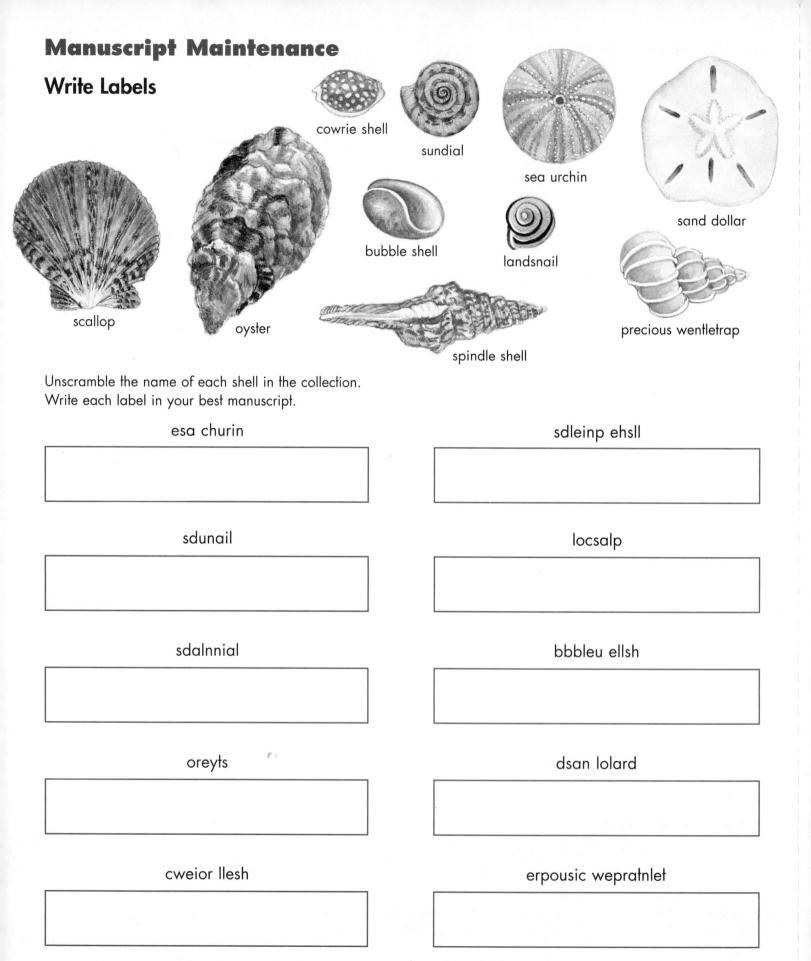

cowrie shell

sundial

sea urchin

sand dollar

bubble shell

landsnail

scallop

oyster

precious wentletrap

spindle shell

Unscramble the name of each shell in the collection.
Write each label in your best manuscript.

esa churin

sdleinp ehsll

sdunail

locsalp

sdalnnial

bbbleu ellsh

oreyts

dsan lolard

cweior llesh

erpousic wepratnlet

Keys to Legibility  Spacing

Follow these guidelines to write with good spacing.

Between Letters   There should be space for O.

Between Words   There should be space for \.

Between Sentences   There should be space for O.

Thanksgiving is an American holiday! The first Thanksgiving was in 1621.

Write these lines about the first Thanksgiving.
To maintain correct spacing, be sure to shift your paper as you write.

We began to gather in the small harvest we had. We started to fit up our dwellings against winter. Our first winter was harsh.   —adapted from William Bradford's writings, 1621

Spacing

Is there space for O between letters?   Yes   No

Is there space for \ between words?   Yes   No

Is there space for O between sentences?   Yes   No

Write Greetings

Every language has words used to greet people.

	Hello	**Good-bye**
French	bonjour	au revoir
Spanish	hola	hasta la vista
German	guten Tag	auf wiedersehen
Italian	buon giorno	ciao
Swahili	jambo	kwahire
Chinese	nei ho	joi gin
Turkish	merhaba	güle güle

1. Write hello and good-bye in Spanish. Use cursive writing.

2. Write hello and good-bye in Italian. Use cursive writing.

3. Write hello and good-bye in French. Use cursive writing.

4. Write hello and good-bye in Swahili. Use cursive writing.

5. Write hello and good-bye in Chinese. Use cursive writing.

Write your family's favorite way to say hello and good-bye.

Spacing

Is your spacing between letters correct?	Yes	No
Is your writing easy to read?	Yes	No

Write a List

Lists help to organize important ideas.
Here is a list of endangered species and where they live.

Species	Areas
giant armadillo	Venezuela, Guyana to Argentina
bobcat	United States, Canada, Mexico
American crocodile	U.S., Mexico, Caribbean Sea, Central and South America
Asian elephant	South central and Southeastern Asia
gorilla	Central and West Africa
kangaroo	Australia
lion	Africa, India
orangutan	Borneo, Sumatra

Choose four species you would like to help save.
List the species and the countries in which they live. Use cursive handwriting.

1. _____

2. _____

3. _____

4. _____

DID YOU KNOW?

About 900 species of animals that live in America are endangered.

Did you use correct spacing between words?	Yes	No
Is your writing easy to read?	Yes	No

Write a Poem

Many people write poems for fun and to learn more about themselves.
Write a poem about yourself by answering each of the questions below. Use your best cursive writing.

A "Me" Poem

Line 1. Your first name only

_____

_____

Line 2. Who likes (3 words)

_____

_____

Line 3. Who does not like (3 words)

_____

_____

Line 4. Who is good at (3 words)

_____

_____

Line 5. Who spends time (3 words)

_____

_____

Line 6. Who wants to learn (3 words)

_____

_____

Line 7. Who wants to be (3 words)

_____

_____

Line 8. Your last name only

_____

_____

Is your spacing between letters correct?		Yes	No
Is your writing easy to read?		Yes	No

Keys to Legibility  Slant

Follow these suggestions to write with uniform slant.

POSITION
PULL
SHIFT

• Check your paper position.

• Pull your downstrokes in the proper direction.

• Shift your paper as you write.

If you are left-handed . . .

pull toward your left elbow.

If you are right-handed . . .

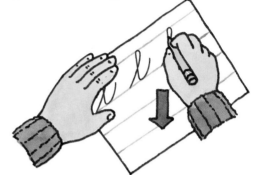

pull toward your midsection.

Write the names of these American inventors, their inventions, and the year. Use cursive writing.

Benjamin Franklin, bifocal lenses, 1780

George Eastman, camera, 1888

Robert Jarvik, artifical heart, 1982

Mary Anderson, windshield wiper, 1904

Sarah Boone, ironing board, 1892

 Slant

Check your slant.
Draw lines through the slant strokes of the letters.

Your slant should look like *lllllollll*, not *uniform*.

Write Punctuation Marks

Use these punctuation marks to help clarify your ideas when you write.

. period	? question mark	! exclamation mark
, comma	' apostrophe	" " quotation marks

Write each sentence in cursive. Remember to include punctuation marks.
Pay attention to the slant of your letters as you write.

"Do you like to read stories?" Benita asked.

"Yes! I like mysteries," Rojas exclaimed.

Benita said, "I know a great mystery book. I'll lend it to you."

"Great! I can't wait to read it," Rojas replied.

Write a sentence with at least three punctuation marks.

	Yes	No
Does your writing include correct punctuation?	Yes	No
Does your writing have good slant?	Yes	No

The Writing Process
Write a Story

A short story is a brief work of fiction that contains made-up characters and events.
A story takes place at a specific time and place, called the **setting**.
The action is based around a **plot**, the series of events.

Here are some possible ideas for your story.

> **Imagine you are taking a trip.**
> **Write a story about all the things that happen on your trip.**
>
> **Imagine that you dig up a mysterious trunk.**
> **Write a story about the things you find in that trunk.**

Follow these steps for writing a short story.

I. Prewriting

Start by thinking about a plot for your short story. **Plan** your plot on the following chart.
Write legibly so you can read your ideas later. Use cursive writing.

Setting:

Characters:

Problem:

Events:

Solution:

2. Drafting
Write your first draft.

_____
_____
_____
_____
_____
_____
_____
_____
_____
_____
_____
_____
_____
_____
_____
_____
_____
_____
_____

COLLISION ALERT Make sure that your tall letters do not bump into descenders above them.

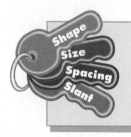

Does your writing have good shape?	Yes	No
Does your writing have good size?	Yes	No
Does your writing have good spacing?	Yes	No
Does your writing have good slant?	Yes	No

3. Revising

Read your draft and mark any changes you want to make. You may want
to ask a classmate to help you. Use editing marks as you revise your short story.

Use these proofreading marks to edit your writing.

☰	Capitalize.	∧	Insert or add.
/	Use lowercase.	ℓ	Delete or take out.
⊙	Add a period.	⊤	Indent for a new paragraph.

4. Editing

Check your story for errors in spelling, punctuation, capitalization, and handwriting.
Answer the questions below to help you edit your story.
You may want to ask a classmate to help you.

Is your story interesting?	Yes	No
Does the ending make sense?	Yes	No
Does your story include dialogue?	Yes	No
Are all the words spelled correctly?	Yes	No
Did you avoid collisions?	Yes	No
Do your letters rest on the baseline?	Yes	No
Are short letters half the height of tall letters?	Yes	No
Is there good spacing between letters, words, and sentences?	Yes	No
Does your writing have uniform slant?	Yes	No
Is your writing legible?	Yes	No

5. Publishing

In your best handwriting, make a clean copy of your story.
Then follow these steps to publish your story:

• Add a title and your name.

• Add an illustration, if you wish.

• Read your story to a small group of classmates.

Manuscript Maintenance

A Homework Plan

Make a homework plan for next week. Write the information in the sample, or make up a plan of your own. Use manuscript writing.

Day	Subject	Time	Materials
Monday	Reading—pages 43-50	7:00	Island of the Blue Dolphins
Tuesday	Spelling—write words in sentences	8:00	Spelling word list page 36
Wednesday	Reading—pages 51-53 Math—top of page 42	6:30 7:30	Island of the Blue Dolphins
Thursday	Social Studies—plan project with partner Spelling—spell words aloud	3:30 4:30	Daniel Boone biography
Friday—Saturday	Art—finish Boonesborough	all Saturday afternoon	Sticks, glue, brown paint

Day	Subject	Time	Materials

On another piece of paper, write the first stanza of this American folk song in your best cursive handwriting.

This Land Is Your Land

This land is your land, this land is my land

From California to the New York island,

From the redwood forest to the Gulf Stream waters

This land was made for you and me.

As I was walking that ribbon of highway,

I saw above me that endless skyway,

I saw below me that golden valley

This land was made for you and me.

Woody Guthrie

Writing Quickly

Writing quickly is a skill that will help when you need to draft a story, write during a timed test, or take notes as your teacher talks. Writing that is done quickly should still be easy to read. With practice, you will learn how to make your writing speedy and legible.

Read the quotation below. Write it quickly and legibly.

Remember that a journey of a thousand miles begins with a single step.

Write the saying again. Try to write it faster, but make sure your writing is legible.

Write the saying two more times. Try to write it even faster, but keep it easy to read.

Now read your writing. Circle Yes or No to respond to each statement. Then show your writing to another reader, either a classmate or your teacher. Ask that person to circle Yes or No beside each statement.

	My Evaluation		My Classmate's or Teacher's Evaluation	
The writing is easy to read.	Yes	No	Yes	No
The writing has good **Shape**.	Yes	No	Yes	No
The writing has good **Size**.	Yes	No	Yes	No
The writing has good **Spacing**.	Yes	No	Yes	No
The writing has good **Slant**.	Yes	No	Yes	No

Writing Easily

As you write stories and essays for school papers and tests, it is important that your handwriting flows easily. When you automatically know how to write legibly, you don't have to worry about your handwriting. You are free to think about what you want your writing to say. With practice, you will learn how to make your writing easy, quick, and legible.

Read the writing prompt below. Respond to it by writing on the lines. Let your handwriting flow easily as you think and write.

Ballot
Vote for one

Mary ☐
Anton ☐
Pat ☒

Persuasive Writing

Pretend you are running for president of your class.

Write a paragraph that will persuade your classmates to vote for you. Include details about what you would do as president and why you are a good candidate.

VOTE HERE

Now read your writing. Circle Yes or No to respond to each statement. Then show your writing to another reader, either a classmate or your teacher. Ask that person to circle Yes or No beside each statement.

	My Evaluation		My Classmate's or Teacher's Evaluation	
The writing is easy to read.	Yes	No	Yes	No
The writing has good Shape.	Yes	No	Yes	No
The writing has good Size.	Yes	No	Yes	No
The writing has good Spacing.	Yes	No	Yes	No
The writing has good Slant.	Yes	No	Yes	No

Handwriting and the Writing Process
Write a Paragraph

A paragraph is a group of sentences about a main idea.
Write a paragraph about your favorite holiday and how you celebrate it.

1. Prewriting

Prewriting means gathering ideas and planning before you write.
List your ideas on a piece of paper. Then plan your paragraph, telling the
subject and in what order you will write your ideas.

2. Drafting

Drafting means putting your thoughts into written sentences for the first time.
Use the ideas you listed in Prewriting to draft your paragraph. Write your
first draft.

3. Revising

Revising means changing your writing to make it say exactly what you
mean. Read your draft. Mark any changes you want to make.

Does your writing include all the information readers want to know?   Yes   No

Does your writing include descriptive details?   Yes   No

4. Editing

Editing means checking your revised writing for errors in spelling,
punctuation, capitalization, and handwriting.

Are all words spelled correctly?   Yes   No

Have you used uppercase letters and punctuation correctly?   Yes   No

Do your letters have good shape and size?   Yes   No

Is there good spacing between letters, words, and sentences?   Yes   No

Does your writing have good uniform slant?   Yes   No

Is your writing easy to read?   Yes   No

5. Publishing

Publishing means using your best handwriting to make an error-free
copy of your writing. Share your writing.

Record of Student's Handwriting Skills

Cursive

	Needs Improvement	Shows Mastery
Sits correctly	☐	☐
Holds pencil correctly	☐	☐
Positions paper correctly	☐	☐
Writes numerals 1–10	☐	☐
Writes undercurve letters: **i, t, u, w, e, l, b, h**	☐	☐
Writes undercurve letters: **f, k, r, s, j, p**	☐	☐
Writes downcurve letters: **a, d, g, o, c, q**	☐	☐
Writes overcurve letters: **n, m, y, x, v, z**	☐	☐
Writes downcurve letters: **A, O, D, C, E**	☐	☐
Writes curve forward letters: **N, M, H, K, U, Y, Z, V, W, X**	☐	☐
Writes overcurve letters: **I, J, Q**	☐	☐
Writes doublecurve letters: **T, F**	☐	☐
Writes undercurve-loop letters: **G, S, L**	☐	☐
Writes undercurve-slant letters: **P, R, B**	☐	☐
Writes the undercurve to undercurve joining	☐	☐
Writes the undercurve to downcurve joining	☐	☐
Writes the undercurve to overcurve joining	☐	☐
Writes the overcurve to undercurve joining	☐	☐
Writes the overcurve to downcurve joining	☐	☐
Writes the overcurve to overcurve joining	☐	☐
Writes the checkstroke to undercurve joining	☐	☐
Writes the checkstroke to downcurve joining	☐	☐
Writes the checkstroke to overcurve joining	☐	☐
Writes with correct shape	☐	☐
Writes with correct size	☐	☐
Writes with correct spacing	☐	☐
Writes with uniform slant	☐	☐
Writes quickly	☐	☐
Writes with ease	☐	☐
Regularly checks written work for legibility	☐	☐

Index